I CAN BE A WRITER

I Can Be a Script Writer

Meeg Pincus

Published in the United States of America by:

Cherry Lake Press
2395 South Huron Parkway, Suite 200, Ann Arbor, Michigan 48104
www.cherrylakepress.com

Reading Adviser: Beth Walker Gambro, MS, Ed., Reading Consultant, Yorkville, IL

Photo Credits: © Fabio Pagani/Dreamstime.com, 5; © Seventyfourimages/Dreamstime.com, 6; © bombermoon/shutterstock, 7; © Ken Wolter/Dreamstime.com, 8 (left); © James Kirkikis/Dreamstime.com, 8 (right); © Dimabl/Dreamstime.com, 11; © Mykhailo Polenok/Dreamstime.com, 12; © Media_Photos/Shutterstock, 13; © Pixelbliss/Shutterstock, 14; © Wirestock/Dreamstime.com, 15; © Ariya J/Shutterstock, 16; © smolaw/Shutterstock, 18; © CREATISTA/Shutterstock, 20; © Fabio Pagani/Dreamstime.com, 22

Copyright © 2026 by Cherry Lake Publishing Group

All rights reserved. No part of this book may be reproduced or utilized in any form or by any means without written permission from the publisher.

Cherry Lake Press is an imprint of Cherry Lake Publishing Group.

Names: Pincus, Meeg author
Title: I can be a script writer / by Meeg Pincus.
Description: Ann Arbor, Michigan : Cherry Lake Publishing, 2025. | Series: I can be a writer | Audience: Grades 2-3 | Summary: "Are you ready to bring your story to the big screen? Readers are welcomed into the world of scriptwriting as they connect their growing writing skills with the work professionals out in the world do. In this series by award-winning author Meeg Pincus, young writers can learn what it takes to write like a professional. From scriptwriter to book author, students get a sneak peek at what their future may hold and the skills they can practice today to get them there"— Provided by publisher.
Identifiers: LCCN 2025009295 | ISBN 9781668963609 hardcover | ISBN 9781668964927 paperback | ISBN 9781668966532 ebook | ISBN 9781668968147 pdf
Subjects: LCSH: Motion picture authorship—Vocational guidance—Juvenile literature
Classification: LCC PN1996 .P59 2025 | DDC 808.2/3—dc23/eng/20250313
LC record available at https://lccn.loc.gov/2025009295

Cherry Lake Publishing Group would like to acknowledge the work of the Partnership for 21st Century Learning, a Network of Battelle for Kids. Please visit Battelle for Kids online for more information.

Printed in the United States of America

Note from publisher: Websites change regularly, and their future contents are outside of our control. Supervise children when conducting any recommended online searches for extended learning opportunities.

CONTENTS

What Do Script Writers Do?	4
Why Would I Want to Write Scripts?	10
How Can I Learn to Write Scripts?	17
Activity	22
Find Out More	23
About the Author	23
Glossary	24
Index	24

WHAT DO SCRIPT WRITERS DO?

Do you like to watch movies or TV shows? Do you enjoy going to live stage plays or musicals? Are there favorite lines you like to repeat from your favorite **productions**?

Then you have seen and heard what script writers do!

Script writers write the text of a film, television show, or stage play. Playwrights write scripts for the stage. Screenwriters write scripts for film and TV.

Scripts include the characters, plot, and setting of films and TV shows.

Script writers craft the **narrative** story of a show. They also write all the words, or **dialogue**, every character speaks.

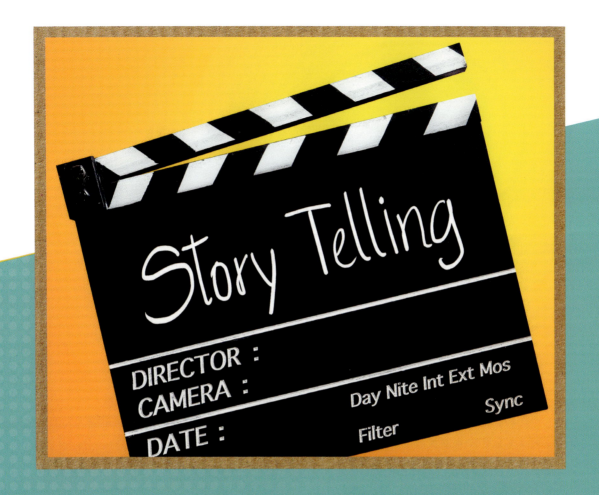

Many script writers come up with their own story ideas. Sometimes they may adapt a book or a real-life story into a script.

Some script writers work for one film studio or theater and write just for them. Many script writers work on their own and sell their scripts to different places.

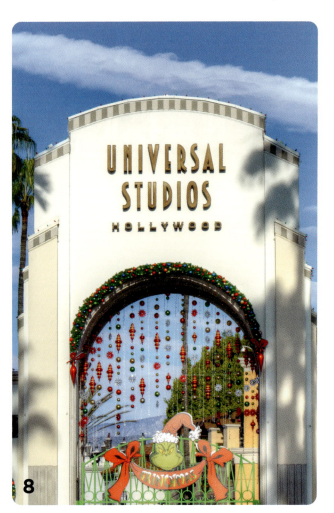
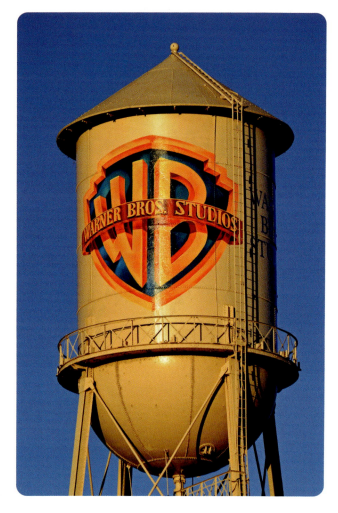

Some write scripts based on the story ideas of people who hire them.

Look!

Look! Watch a favorite movie or TV show. Pause on a scene you love. Rewatch the scene a few times. Pay attention to the words the actors say—that's the script!

Some script writers adapt stories from comics.

9

WHY WOULD I WANT TO WRITE SCRIPTS?

When you think up stories, do you imagine scenes that include costumes, sets, and sound effects? Do you love the idea of writing words that will be read out loud by actors?

Then you may want to write scripts!

Think!

What do your favorite scenes in plays, films, or TV shows have in common? What kind of words make a scene feel powerful to you? Are they funny or dramatic? Loud or quiet?

Film and TV crews can include hundreds of people.

Does the idea of working with a team of people to create something together sound exciting? As a script writer, you get to see performers, artists, and **technicians** bring your words to life.

Scripts are the first important piece of any production. You get to be part of a bigger piece of art.

Your job as a script writer is not writing lots of detailed descriptions of places or people. You get to focus on your characters' words, feelings, and actions.

As a script writer, you think about why your characters want things. You think about what they might do to move your story forward. Then you put those thoughts into words that sound like real conversations.

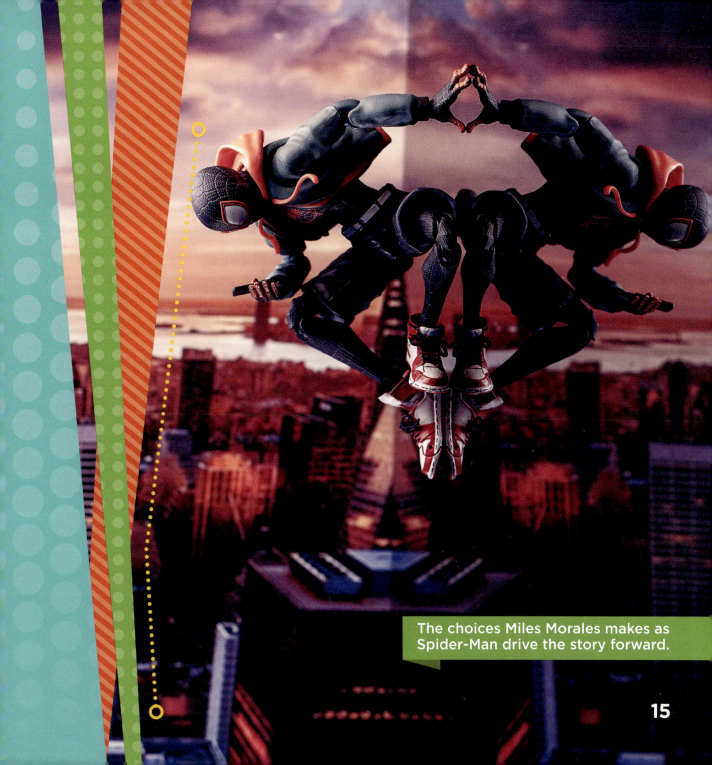

The choices Miles Morales makes as Spider-Man drive the story forward.

HOW CAN I LEARN TO WRITE SCRIPTS?

Do you know you can get the original scripts of many of your favorite movies, TV shows, and plays? Reading many scripts helps you learn how to write them.

You can study how to **format** scripts. And you can see how a script writer's words on the page sound when actors speak them.

Storyboards help filmmakers visualize scenes in a script.

18

To be a script writer, you learn to come up with an interesting story and cast of characters. Then you learn to break down your story into scenes.

You can practice writing dialogue between characters in your own stories. You can try writing extra scenes for films, shows, and plays you love.

Make a Guess!

Script writers need to make sure the words they write will sound good when actors say them out loud. How do you think they do that?

Youth theater is a great way to learn about storytelling.

You can take classes in scriptwriting and story writing. Playwrights usually study **drama** as well. They can enter contests to have their plays produced by theaters. Screenwriters usually also study filmmaking.

Can you be a script writer? If you want to learn to write stories, characters, and dialogue for stage or screen ... yes, you can!

Ask Questions!

Find the name of the script writer for a film, show, or play you like. Then write them a letter. Ask what they like about writing scripts. Ask how they knew they wanted to write scripts. Ask any questions you have for them!

ACTIVITY

Pick two or more characters from a favorite book. Write a scene in which they are talking with each other. Give the conversation a story, including a beginning, middle, and end.

You can format it like this:

SETTING: Write where they are (such as the library, the zoo, or a Martian colony).

CHARACTER 1: Write what they say.

CHARACTER 2: Write what they say.

FIND OUT MORE

Books

Prentice, Andrew, and Matthew Oldham. *Write Your Own Scripts.* London, UK: Usborne, 2023.

Stemple, Heidi E. Y. *Janie Writes a Play*. Watertown, MA: Charlesbridge, 2025.

Websites

With an adult, explore more online with these suggested searches.

"Disney Scripts Collection: Television and Screenplays Download," *Bulletproof Screenwriting*

"Reader's Theater Editions," *Aaron Shepard* site

ABOUT THE AUTHOR

Meeg Pincus loves to write. She is the author of more than 30 books for children. She has been a writer and editor for books, newspapers, magazines, and more. She also loves to sing, make art, and hang out with her family, friends, and adorable dog.

GLOSSARY

dialogue (DYE-uh-lahg) conversation between two or more characters in a play or film

drama (DRAH-muh) theater arts

format (FOHR-mat) structure in which something is arranged and presented

narrative (NAIR-uh-tiv) having the form of a story, with a plot, setting, and characters

productions (pruh-DUK-shuhns) works or shows presented to the public

scene (SEEN) single situation in a story or production

technicians (tek-NIH-shuhns) people skilled at a mechanical job, such as lighting or sound

INDEX

activities, 21, 22
adaptations, 7, 9

characters, 6, 14–15, 19, 21, 22
crews, 12–13

dialogue, 6, 9, 10, 11, 14, 17, 19, 21, 22

education, 17, 19, 21

film writing, 4–5, 8, 9, 10–12, 17, 20
formatting, 5, 16, 17, 18

learning, 17–21

plots, 6–7, 9, 14–15, 19, 21

reading habits, 17

script writers, 4–9, 10–14, 17–21
storyboards, 18

teamwork, 12
technicians, 12–13
theater and drama, 4, 8, 17, 20–21
TV writing, 4–5, 9, 10–12, 17

writing scripts, 4–9, 10–14, 16–21, 22

youth theater, 20